599
STE

Steiner, Barbara A.

Biography of a
desert bighorn

DATE			
NOV 3 19?? APR 17 1980			
DEC 1 ? 1978			
FEB 1 4 1979			
MAY 9 ??			
NOV DEC 12 ??			
JAN 1 8 1980			
OCT 6 198?			

About the Book

Above the dry, Southwestern desert and the vast stretches of harsh fallen rock, Little Ewe gives birth. She runs her warm black tongue over the eight-pound, chocolate-brown baby ram. Already he is able to stagger up on his wobbly legs—legs which will soon learn to traverse the most jagged and treacherous rock in places where only the desert bighorn can safely go.

This warm, sensitive portrayal of the desert bighorn shows the animals in their natural habitat from birth to often untimely death. This is the story of Little Ewe and her ram, Beju, but it is as well a tale of survival.

Barbara Steiner writes with compassion, humor and simplicity. She gives us a moving story of one animal's fight for existence in a rugged and often brutal wasteland.

Biography of a
DESERT BIGHORN

by Barbara Steiner

ILLUSTRATED BY LINDA POWELL

G. P. Putnam's Sons   New York

ACKNOWLEDGMENTS

Thank you to Lanny O. Wilson, wildlife biologist, who was helpful in answering many questions, and who helped me locate material without which this book could not have been written.

To those people who unselfishly devote much of their time in an effort to save the endangered species and to Dr. Charles Hansen, who gave his life in studying the desert bighorn.

One winter day on a dry southwestern desert a small herd of bighorn sheep fed at the base of a cliff. All the sheep were females except one. He was Brownie, Little Ewe's lamb from a year ago. Little Ewe left the bighorn sheep herd. Slowly she began to climb the steep, rocky slope. Brownie started to follow her. She lowered her head and butted him away. She wanted to be alone when her new lamb was born.

Little Ewe plodded upward, picking her way between fallen rocks. She felt heavy and restless. The baby she had carried inside her body for six months was also restless. Kick. Kick. His small hooves pounded against her sides.

She reached the sunny slopes of the lambing ground. The area was dotted with loose rock. This made walking dangerous for anyone except a bighorn sheep. Little Ewe could see for a long distance. It was a safe place to have her baby.

She chose a spot in the early-morning sunshine. She pawed out a shallow bed and knelt down. Her baby was born on the warm, sandy soil.

The baby bighorn weighed eight pounds. Little Ewe was sandy-colored, but her baby was covered with chocolate brown hair. The hair on his rump was yellowish, and his nose was white.

Little Ewe ran her warm black tongue over the lamb, Beju. She cleaned him from head to toe. Her breath was warm. She uttered low grunts of pleasure as she licked him.

Already Beju was an independent lamb. He staggered up on his wobbly legs. Oops! Down he fell against Little Ewe. He nosed her soft warmth and found the delicious taste of warm milk. Happily he pushed his rump into the air. He wagged his tiny tail as he began to nurse.

Beju nursed for only a few seconds. Then Little Ewe nuzzled him down into the warm bed. She climbed a cliff above where her lamb lay and curled up in the warm sunshine.

When Beju woke, he watched for Little Ewe with his large dark eyes. But he didn't move from the place where she had left him. Before he was born, Beju's tiny white hooves were soft so he would not hurt his mother when he kicked. By the time Little Ewe returned Beju's hooves had hardened. He stood up and started to nurse without wobbling.

Beju felt frisky after he had eaten. He backed up with a bounce. He didn't see the ephedra bush that grew close to his bed. He toppled into it.

Beju bleated as Little Ewe walked away, but she didn't help Beju. He pulled and scrambled. Finally he struggled to his feet. Skipping back to his bed, he curled up and fell asleep.

All day Beju slept and nursed. He was stronger each time Little Ewe returned to him. Once he started to follow her. Little Ewe put her head against his side and gently pushed him off his feet.

Bleating, Beju sprawled on the ground. Quickly he scrambled to his feet and ran toward her. Again she shoved him down. Again he popped back up. He liked this new game. But soon Beju was tired. He forgot to get up. He put his head down and went to sleep right where he had fallen.

By the end of a week Beju played while his
mother grazed. He was nursing less often and
and cut several teeth. Running over to Little
Ewe, he put his nose to the ground where she
snipped off sprigs of the bebbia plant.

Not many plants grew in this land of sun and
little water, but bighorn can eat almost

anything. Little Ewe held out a tender twig to
Beju. Carefully he nibbled off a bite for himself.
This was good. He began to eat alongside Little
Ewe.

Beju loved to play. Sometimes he would run
around in circles. Then he would butt his small
head against a rock or bush or even his mother.
One day Beju decided to explore. He left his
mother and bravely walked up the
mountainside. His ears were forward. He held
his head high.

All of a sudden right in front of him stood a large chuckwalla lizard. Startled, the chuckwalla dashed for a crack between two rocks. Beju whirled around. His ears came down. His bravery vanished.

"Baaa, baaa." His frightened bleats echoed down the canyon walls. Running, he looked this way and that. Just as he fell over a large rock, he

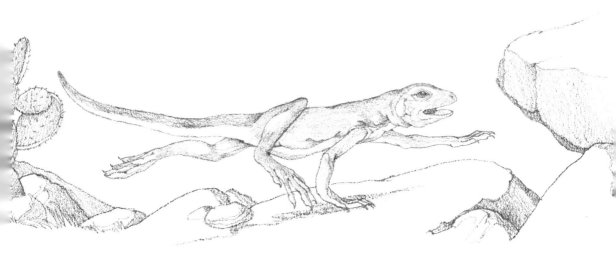

saw his mother. She was chewing her cud in the warm sunshine.

He wagged his tail and ran to her. "Baaa, baaa." He touched his small nose to hers and cuddled close to her. Exploring was over, at least until tomorrow.

By the time Beju was a month old he weighed twelve pounds. His rump patch was changing from yellowish brown to snow white like his mother's. The bumps on his head had pushed his hair up, but no tiny horns had broken through the skin. Walking miles up and down the mountainside for water every day had made his legs strong.

15

One morning they walked quickly, not
stopping to eat. Soon Beju grew tired and could
not keep up. He lay down in the shade of a
mesquite bush and watched Little Ewe stop to
browse. She moved from plant to plant, a bite
here, a nibble there, slowly continuing down the
mountain.

16

Few large animals lived in the harsh desert
land. The bighorn sheep had almost no enemies.
Beju was hidden as he napped by the bush. He
had no scent. But today he was unlucky.

An old coyote was heading down the
mountain for water. He would have passed by
where Beju was sleeping, but he stumbled over a
loose rock. It tumbled down the mountain. Beju
jumped up and started to bleat, "Baaa, baaa."

Then he saw the coyote. The coyote stared at
Beju. Because Beju was alone, the coyote closed
in to attack.

Quickly Beju turned and headed back up the slope. In front of him a large slippery rock slanted almost straight up. But Beju kept going. Up, up, up the rock he climbed. His sturdy little legs never wobbled. His hooves had soft rubbery inner pads that gripped and clung to the slick rock.

With a leap he landed on a tiny ledge. The coyote looked up. He couldn't climb the steep rock. Beju was safe.

For some time Beju and the coyote stared at each other. Then the coyote went on down the mountain. Beju folded his long legs under him and settled on the ledge for another nap.

When he woke, it was getting dark. Where was his mother? His unhappy bleat filled the cold night air. Finally he scrambled down the slick rock. He pawed out a small bed between two large rocks and lay down for the night.

Morning came, and Beju's mother was still not there. Beju wandered unhappily, bleating for her. Sometimes he nibbled at plants or bushes, but he was thirsty and lonesome. Off and on during the day he napped. Then he pawed out a bed under a overhanging rock for the night.

On the second day Beju was still alone. He ran and searched. His small bleat never stopped unless he fell asleep.

Toward evening on the third day, he entered a dry wash at the base of the mountain. "Baaa, baaa," he called.

Then he heard a deep answer, "Baaa, baaa." He ran faster.

Beju raced between two huge boulders and came out into an open space where several sheep were grazing. Surely one of these sheep was his mother. He bounced to an old bighorn ewe with a broken horn and tried to nurse. No, this wasn't his mother.

But Little Ewe was there. She had returned to her year-old lamb, Brownie, and the herd of females led by Old Ewe. Little Ewe made a burping sound. Beju bounded to meet her. They touched noses, and Beju settled down to eat. The warm milk tasted good. His frisky tail wagged around and around. Little Ewe mewed in a small voice as Beju nursed.

After eating, Beju set out to explore. He had never seen any sheep except his mother, but he wasn't afraid. First he butted his small head into Brownie. Brownie turned and shoved him over.

Bobbing to his feet, he ran to touch noses with two lambs. Little Bek was a week younger and Tika was two weeks older than Beju. Beju had found not only his mother but two friends. What a happy day!

The three lambs jumped and leaped. Soon the whole herd was running and leaping. Brownie butted Little Ewe, who jumped and turned around in midair. Bounce, hop, spin, and turn, the sheep played. Beju butted Old Ewe. She joined the fun as she danced in a circle. Then she jumped on a large rock to watch.

Beju would not know his father. The male bighorn sheep, called rams, live apart from the females. They travel the desert in small groups or alone during the winter, spring, and early summer.

Winter days turned to spring, and the sun became hotter. Some years flowers would bloom on the desert floor and up the gullies that led to the steep mountain. But this was a dry year, and not many new green leaves appeared. Those that did were hunted down and enjoyed by the browsing sheep.

In winter ewes who were not nursing could go for two weeks without water. But now the herd stayed close to the water hole. The bighorn looked shaggy. They rubbed against rocks and bushes. They were shedding old hair and growing new, giving them a thick coat to protect them against the hot sun.

Each day the herd wandered up the gullies leading to the mountain. They ate and rested in the shade of bushes. They spent the night high on the mountain. Early in the morning they returned to the water.

Beju, Little Bek, and Tika became best friends. They were always together. They raced and frolicked across the rocky ground. Sometimes Little Bek couldn't keep up. He stopped because of a cough which wracked his small body. His coat was rough, and his ribs showed. Still he tried to join in the games.

One morning the herd came down the mountain from a different direction. Beju bounced behind Old Ewe as she led them to a spring about three miles from Mesquite Spring. Small Spring was a favorite place for picnickers and campers as it was close to a main road. The thistle, Old Ewe's favorite food, grew nearby. The herd would water and browse if there were no people. But today the bighorn would find no water in Small Spring.

A family had camped there overnight. While the parents packed, three children played by throwing rocks in Small Spring to see the water splash. It had never been a large water hole. Only small puddles were left, and they had dried up quickly in the thirsty sun.

Beju watched Little Ewe paw a rock aside and try to suck up water from the damp ground. He tried digging, too. He couldn't get any water.

While the sheep nibbled at the thistle plants,
Beju led the lambs around the campsite. Being
young, they would sample food which didn't
interest the adults. Little Bck licked a baked
bean can left in the fireplace. Beju ate a paper
bag dropped by one of the children. Then Tika
found something that smelled quite different.
She sniffed it curiously.

Father had taken a picture before he left. He had thrown the black backing from the film to the ground. Tika nosed it around. Beju wanted it. He butted Tika away. But Little Bek knocked Beju over backward. Before Beju could get up, he saw Tika gobble up the black paper.

Beju noticed the herd was leaving. So the lambs hurried to catch up. They followed Old Ewe across the open desert back to Mesquite Spring.

Within two days Tika was ill. Beju challenged her, but she would not bump heads with him. Little Bek whirled in circles, but Tika only watched.

One morning Tika bleated a sharp cry. She sat down. She couldn't run after Beju and Little Bek. Beju danced back to touch noses with Tika. Then he ran to keep up with the herd, who were seeking shelter for their morning nap.

The chemical on the film backing was poison to the small lamb. Tika was left alone to die from eating the paper the careless camper had thrown away.

By July Beju was six months old. He had stopped nursing. He stood a little over two feet tall and weighed sixty-five pounds. His small pointed horns were six inches long. He delighted in hitting them against bushes, rocks, and Little Bek.

Often the two lambs stood on their hind feet. They cocked heads sideways. Taking a few wobbly steps toward each other, they bumped horns as their forefeet dropped to the ground. This was an endless game, except when Little Bek stopped to cough. Then Beju would challenge Brownie.

Little Bek's cough was getting worse. More and more he had to rest. Now the lambs played early or late in the day as the desert sun sent temperatures over one hundred degrees by noon.

Brownie taught them to play King of the
Mountain. Jumping onto a boulder, he lowered
his head and stamped his foot. Both lambs
would try to get onto the rock. Once Beju
jumped up from behind and knocked Brownie
off. But Brownie was as large as his mother.
Quickly he pushed Beju off and gained his
mountain again.

Early one day in August before the sun claimed the day for its own, an unusual thing happened. Two large rams with huge curled horns were waiting at Mesquite Spring. The dark red ram butted Little Ewe in the side when she tried to drink.

Beju lay down to watch, but Brownie seemed excited. He pawed the ground, snorted, and danced toward the other bighorn. Old Ram paid no attention to Brownie.

Beju didn't know what was happening, but this was the beginning of the mating season for that year. Now, and through the fall months, the male bighorn would live with the females. Old Ram might be Beju's father, but he had nothing to do with raising the lambs. Now the rams would mate with the ewes so there could be new lambs again in late winter.

Suddenly a noise startled the bighorn. Quickly Beju jumped up. He joined his herd and the two rams, who had run from the spring. They waited, heads close together and held high. They sniffed the air and looked around, but Old Ewe would decide what to do.

Old Ewe made a rasping sound like two rocks scraped together. She pawed the ground and blew a warning noise through her nose. Quickly she scrambled up a nearby slope and ran.

One by one the herd followed. Their footing was sure as they climbed the loose rock and leaped onto narrow ledges. Dodging a falling rock, Beju hurried to keep up.

Down at the spring the cause of their fear watched them through his binoculars. He would follow. It wasn't hunting season. But this man was a poacher, coming to shoot a bighorn ram when he pleased. He would sell the trophy horns. Slowly he climbed the slope where the bighorn had run so quickly.

Beju was glad to rest while Old Ewe stopped to watch. Her eyes were like the hunter's binoculars. She saw the movement as the man

started to climb behind them. With a snort she led the herd on. They topped the crest of a ridge. Beju raced to keep up. Then, dropping into a ravine, the bighorn started a stiff-legged bound. Little Bek had fallen behind in a fit of coughing. Now he caught up as the sheep slowed their pace.

Beju wanted to stop when they reached the foot of another peak, but Old Ewe never slowed down. Up, up, up, she climbed a steep rock. Then she leaped onto loose gravel, which rattled down the slope behind her. Beju slipped; then he followed as his small hooves gripped the loose rocks.

Even Little Bek climbed the slanty rock. But
he was caught in the loose gravel which slid
down behind the herd. Bleating, he fell down
and into a small pocket between two boulders.
His leg was broken. He could travel no more.

Pneumonia had weakened the lamb, causing
him to fall. Now the broken leg would keep him
prisoner until he starved. His sharp bleats
echoed in vain across the mountainside.

Old Ewe trotted along one of the trails she knew on the mountain. All the sheep followed her obediently.

Suddenly she had to stop. Part of the trail had broken off. Where there had been a narrow path was nothing. The only way to go forward was to leap across an open space to the rock on the other side. It was a long jump, even for a bighorn.

Beju watched Old Ewe walk back and forth. She looked down at the distant rock. Then she looked back down the trail.

She backed up from the cliff's edge. Then she ran forward. Jumping, she dropped off the cliff to the rock below. Her legs bent low to the rock. She got up and walked on for a short distance. Folding her legs under her, she waited.

One by one the bighorn sheep leaped off the cliff to the distant rock below. Then they, too, rested.

Beju looked down. He had never jumped so far. Could he make it? He bleated for his mother to help him. She looked up. She couldn't help Beju. For a few minutes he looked for another way down the cliff. There was no other way or Old Ewe would have taken it. Beju must jump.

He gazed at the rock below. Then he ran forward. He leaped the biggest leap of his short life.

Beju felt his small hooves touch the solid rock below. Springing up like a coil of wire, he danced over to his mother. He folded up his small legs and rested.

Old Ewe didn't rest long. She looked down the mountain. Then she leaped off the rock platform to a tiny ledge below. Not stopping, she bounced off that ledge to a wrinkle in the rock on the other side of the chimneylike formation. Turning in midair like an acrobat, she jumped again. Now she was on solid ground one hundred feet below the herd. She ran on down the talus slope.

All the sheep followed, even Beju. He was now an experienced mountaineer.

The sheep came to rest in an area of sandstone rocks and tiny caves miles from Mesquite Spring and the illegal hunter. He would not find them here. Beju settled on a shady ledge. He was tired after his new experiences.

Toward evening the heat dropped, and a slight breeze wandered across the mountaintop. Old Ram went to stand on a rock overlooking the silent valley below. He held his head high, despite the weight of his massive horns. The tip of one had been broken off in a fight. But the solidly built old ram looked like a real king of the mountain.

Bcju stood looking at him. Then quickly he skipped away. Big Red pawed the ground, curled his lip, and growled. Old Ram stood still looking over the desert. Just as Big Red charged forward, Old Ram turned to meet him. He caught the full blow of Big Red's horns on his own. Yet he never moved backward, or he would have fallen off the cliff.

Then slowly Big Ram stepped down from the rock. He nibbled the dry pointed leaves of a desert holly.

Big Red charged again, and Old Ram whirled to meet the blow. Clonk! The sound echoed down the canyon walls. Such a collision should leave the rams dizzy, but neither was bothered by the blow. A hard knob of spongy tissue at the base of each bighorn's head took up the shock of the crash.

Old Ram rose up on his hind legs and blasted Big Red again. Bonk! The hollow sound delighted Brownie, who leaped up and butted Beju in the ribs. Then Brownie whirled and butted a rock.

The two big rams held their noses side by side and pushed their faces against each other. Then Big Red reached and nipped Old Ram's flank. He butted him on the rump. Around they went, nipping, pushing, snorting, and blowing.

The dust rose as they tore up the dry ground.

After one more halfhearted head-on collision, the two rams walked away. They sat down and started chewing their cuds as if to say, "The show is over for today."

For five days the bighorn stayed away from the water hole, remembering the danger there. Then their thirst forced them to return. Very early one morning Old Ewe led them straight down the mountain and across the desert floor. Near Mesquite Spring, she raised her head. Standing beside her, Beju sniffed the air. A strong scent wafted through the waves of heat. Burro!

Usually the bighorn shared Mesquite Spring with the small herd of wild burros, taking turns to drink. There was water for all. But now no rain had fallen for nearly a year, and there was not enough.

The burros were startled by the nearness of the bighorn. One small grayish brown baby looked up from where he stood in the middle of the spring. His nose was a white patch. "Eee-haw-ee-haw, e-e-e-haw-e," he brayed. But the burros needn't worry. Old Ewe wouldn't lead the herd to the spring until they were gone.

Beju was very thirsty, but he stood beside Old Ewe and waited. Would there be any water left?

Finally the burros chased each other off across the desert. They ran, kicking up their heels.

Burros drink more water than sheep. There was none left for the bighorn. Beju scraped at the wet sand with his hoof. Then he waited, but no puddle filled the hole. He shoved his nose in the damp earth, but it didn't satisfy his thirst.

All around the spring the ground was torn up by the sharp burro hooves. What little grass and brush there had been was pulled up by the roots and trampled down. It was no longer a good place for sheep to find food.

That evening Old Ewe bleated and started up the steep talus slope. Big Red was chasing one of the ewes. Old Ram and another ewe were pawing in the damp sand of the spring. Brownie looked up but stayed where he was. Beju didn't want to leave. He was thirsty. But finally he trotted behind Little Ewe and Old Ewe for what would be a long hard trip.

When it got dark, they stopped on a mesa several miles from Mesquite Spring. Beju pawed out a small bed. It was cool, and they could rest.

Early the next morning they continued on their way. They needed to travel before the fiery sun took over. Old Ewe led down off the bare mesa and into a dry gully. There the sheep stopped to breakfast on desert holly. The plant lived in the drought only by thrusting its roots deep down to search for water.

Beju nibbled at the holly. It satisfied his
hunger, but not his thirst. Looking up, he saw
his old enemy, the coyote. Beju stared at him.
But the coyote would not chase Beju. He was
almost dead from lack of water.

Not a sound filled the hot, dry air. All the
birds had gone. All the lizards had disappeared.
No insects buzzed. The desert in time of no rain
was a place where few animals could survive.

For days the bighorn traveled. They slept at night. They dozed in shady nooks when the desert became a fiery furnace.

Beju trotted along. His breathing was shallow. He panted to try to stay cooler, but his throat was parched. His head hung down. His coat was rough and dull. Every rib showed.

More and more slowly the herd moved. They were all very tired. If they didn't find water soon, they would die.

Then one day they started down a rough slope. There was no playful butting and jumping. Beju fell behind. He felt he couldn't take another step. Why didn't Old Ewe stop to rest? The sun blazed down. Heat waves danced across the desert floor.

Then Old Ewe lifted her head. Beju lifted his head. The smell was not a mistake. Water! Had they found water?

Yes! There was plenty for all. They had stumbled to the spring looking like shriveled raisins. Now, as they drank, each bighorn body began to fill out.

Finally, Beju drank enough. His small stomach stuck out. He wandered into the shade of a mesquite tree and fell asleep.

The sheep would stay close to this new water hole, at least until the summer days cooled.

Beju would soon be a year old. He was almost

as large as Little Ewe. His eyes were changing to
the gold yellow of an adult bighorn. His coat
was lighter brown. His horns were starting to
curl.

He would stay with Little Ewe and Old Ewe
until he was almost three. Then he would leave
to live with other rams in his desert home. He
would father new lambs. He would fight the
ritual battles on mountain slopes. Not until he
was seven would his horns have grown as big as
Old Ram's. But when they did, he would
challenge all rams until he was king of the desert
mountains.

About the Author

Barbara Steiner grew up in Arkansas, where she went to Henderson State Teachers College and received a degree in education. She then moved to Kansas, where she worked as a teacher while studying for her master's at the University of Kansas. A person of numerous interests, Mrs. Steiner is a member of the National Wildlife Society and Audubon Society. She has published in many national magazines and has written two other nature biographies for Putnam's, *Biography of a Polar Bear* and *Biography of a Wolf.* She and her family live in Colorado, where she works as a reading specialist.

About the Artist

Linda Powell was brought up and educated in California. After receiving a degree in fine arts from the Art Center College of Design in Los Angeles, she moved to Colorado, where she now works as an assistant art director. Ms. Powell, a member of the Audubon Society, has many interests, among them tropical fish and animals. She has designed numerous cards, posters, calendars, and books.